UFO Mysteries

By N. B. Grace

The
Child's
World®
www.childsworld.com

Published by The Child's World®
1980 Lookout Drive • Mankato, MN 56003-1705
800-599-READ • www.childsworld.com

For Jessie, Joel, and Cash—keep your eyes on the skies!

ACKNOWLEDGMENTS

The Child's World®: Mary Berendes, Publishing Director

Produced by Shoreline Publishing Group LLC
President / Editorial Director: James Buckley, Jr.
Designer: Tom Carling, carlingdesign.com
Cover Art: Slimfilms
Copy Editor: Beth Adelman

Photo Credits
Cover—Main image, alien, and second craft: Corbis; comet: iStock.
Interior—AP/Wide World: 8-9, 10, 11, 12, 14, 18; Corbis: 15, 26, 28, 29;
iStock: 7, 16; Getty Images: 6, 13, 24; Photos. com: 4, 20, 25.

LIBRARY OF CONGRESS CATALOGING-IN-PUBLICATION DATA

Grace, N. B.
 UFO mysteries / N. B. Grace.
   p. cm. — (Boys rock!)
 Includes bibliographical references and index.
 ISBN 1-59296-738-8 (library bound : alk. paper)
 1. Unidentified flying objects—Sightings and encounters—
Juvenile literature. 2. Human-alien encounters—Juvenile
literature. I. Title. II. Series.
 TL789.2.G73 2006
 001.942—dc22

                                    2006001634

Printed in the United States of America
Mankato, Minnesota
September 2009
PA02022

CONTENTS

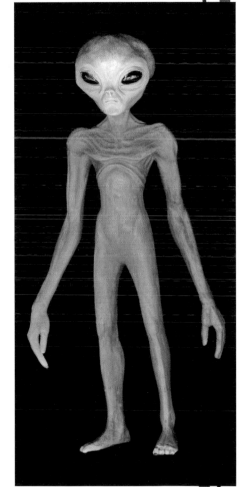

IS ANYONE Out There?

Does life exist on other planets? Have spaceships from distant **galaxies** visited Earth? Could **aliens** ever come to our planet?

These questions have been asked for centuries—but never answered! Even though scientists have not yet discovered life on other planets, they keep looking. Aliens have never been identified, but people keep guessing about them.

In this book, we'll look at the world (or worlds?) of aliens.

OPPOSITE PAGE
Are we alone? There are 100 billion stars in the Milky Way galaxy. How many of them have planets with life on them? No one knows!

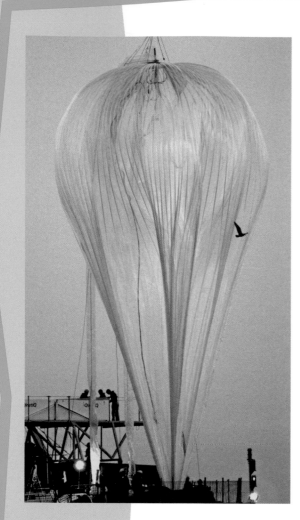

Tall, silvery weather balloons like this one have been confused with UFOs.

Most alien sightings are of UFOs. UFO stands for Unidentified Flying Object. That means someone saw something in the sky that looked . . . weird! What they saw didn't look like a plane or a bird or a cloud (even though all of those have been mistaken for spacecraft). About 95 percent of UFOs turn out to be something normal.

A UFO might turn out to be a weather balloon, a flock of birds, or a plane flying at an odd angle. That still means 5 out of 100 UFOs are unexplained! What are they?

Some people say the UFOs they've seen are shaped like flying saucers.

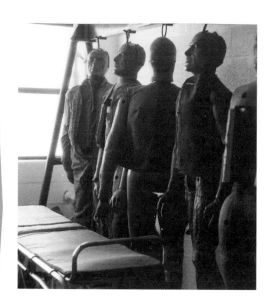

The most famous UFO was spotted in Roswell, New Mexico. No one saw it flying. Instead, it was found after it crashed.

The Air Force said people had confused these test dummies with alien "bodies."

On July 2, 1947, a Roswell rancher heard an explosion during a thunderstorm. When he went out to

Spotting a UFO

Most UFO sightings in the United States happen around 3 a.m. or 9 p.m. They occur more often in July. States in the Northeast and Southwest have the most reported sightings.

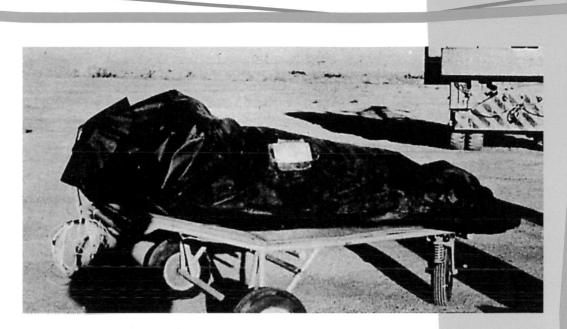

investigate, he found some unusual pieces of wreckage. The pieces were **metallic** but lightweight. The rancher saw some strange symbols on the outside of the pieces.

This black bag holds the pieces of wreckage found at the famous Roswell UFO crash site.

The rancher called the nearby Air Force base. After looking it over, the Air Force said it was a flying saucer!

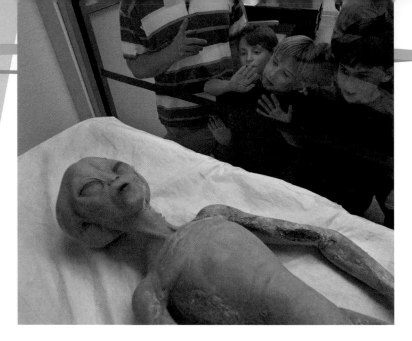

At a museum in Roswell, visitors can look at a plastic model of what some people say the Roswell aliens looked like.

The next day, however, the Air Force changed its story. Officials said that the wreckage was actually a weather balloon being tested by the military.

But was it too late to stop the story? People were sure that aliens had visited Earth. A nurse said she had helped examine the bodies of aliens.

She said they were short, with four fingers on each hand and slits for mouths. No one has found proof that the Roswell stories are true but people still wonder what really happened there.

The Air Force base near Roswell is in what is called Area 51. Today, many UFO research groups work in the area.

There are four types of UFO sightings. Here's how they are divided up:

- Close **Encounter** of the First Kind: Someone sees a UFO (a spacecraft or mysterious lights) flying in the sky.

- Close Encounter of the Second Kind: A UFO appears and leaves behind signs such as burned areas, broken branches, or crop circles (see page 18).

- Close Encounter of the Third Kind: Someone sees a UFO and one or more aliens. A popular movie with this name was made in 1977.

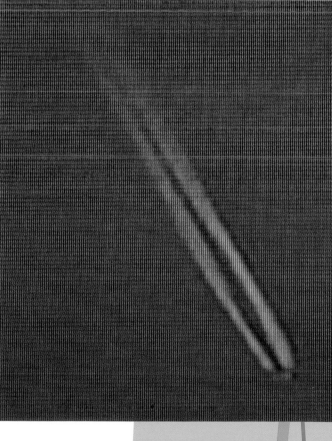

An airplane—or an alien craft? The man who took this photo claimed that it was a UFO!

- Close Encounter of the Fourth Kind: Someone is contacted by aliens and taken on board an alien spacecraft.

Read on to learn more about these so-called alien **abductions**.

In 1961, Betty and Barney Hill claimed that they were abducted while driving at night in the New Hampshire mountains. They said they saw what looked like a bright star darting around their car.

Were the Hills taken aboard an alien spaceship? Or did they make their story up?

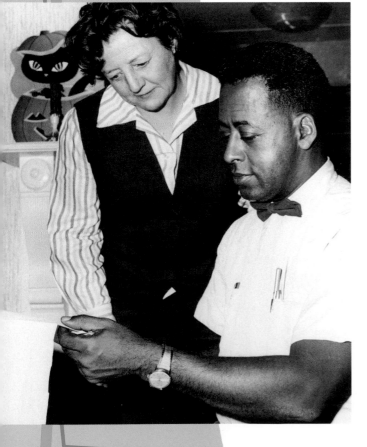

Moments later, they said, they found themselves at home—with no idea how they got there.

Later, under **hypnosis**, the

Is this how the Hills and others were taken on board alien craft? No one knows for sure!

Hills tried to remember what had happened. The Hills said they remembered turning off the highway and seeing aliens standing in the road. The aliens took them aboard their spacecraft, examined them, and asked them questions.

Betty said the aliens were about four and a half feet (about 1 m) tall, with gray skin. She said they had large eyes and slits for mouths. They wore one-piece suits and military caps. Betty said the aliens did not hurt them—in fact, they led the Hills back to their car.

Did it really happen? No one knows. Some people say hypnosis can make people have false memories. Others wonder why the Hills couldn't remember the events without hypnosis.

Whitley Strieber claimed to have been abducted in 1985. He later wrote a popular book about his experience.

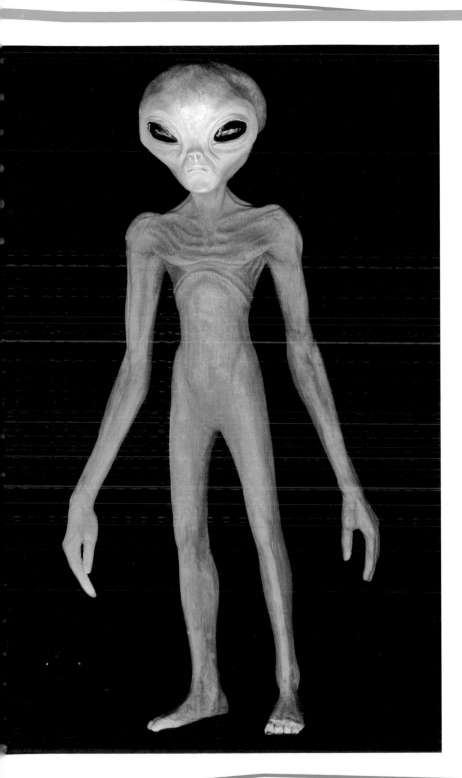

Betty Hill said her alien kidnappers looked like this model.

Some people say alien visitors have left behind mysterious messages— strange crop circles that appear overnight in grassy fields. Crop circles are areas where grasses or crops have been cut or flattened.

Was this pattern in an English wheat field made by aliens—or by people pulling a prank?

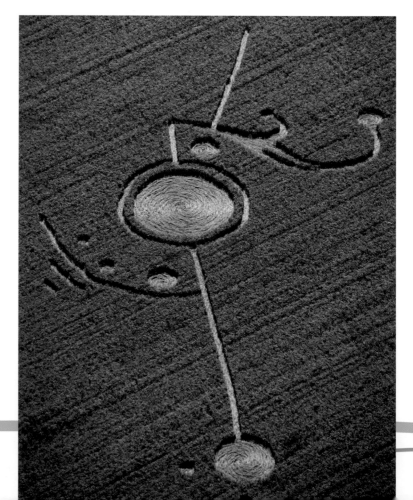

The flattened crops create patterns or shapes. No one is certain how they're made or what they mean.

In the 1980s, hundreds of crop circles began popping up, especially in southern England. A few people have claimed they created the circles as a joke. Others say the circles are too **complicated** for a few people to make overnight. Will the mystery of crop circles be solved one day? For now, they're fun to look at and wonder about.

Complicated is the opposite of simple. Some people believe that making the crop circles was more work than people could do overnight.

OUR SEARCH FOR E.T.

Scientists won't believe in UFOs unless they see proof. They are willing to say that intelligent beings *might* live somewhere else in the universe. The universe is huge, with countless stars like our Sun, and scientists have found signs of planets circling some of those stars.

But scientists still wonder, how many of those planets could have life on them?

If life exists on other planets, is it tiny life forms like **bacteria**? Or are there other kinds of beings that can think and talk—beings like us? To find out, scientists have figured out ways to try to pick up messages that aliens may be sending us right now!

*Is E.T. out there? E.T. stands for **extraterrestrial**, which is another name for aliens.*

Telescopes make distant objects seem closer. Most telescopes pick up light coming from the objects. Others pick up invisible radio waves. **Astronomers** use radio telescopes to study outer space.

What if aliens use radio waves, too? Scientists conducting the Search for Extraterrestrial Intelligence (SETI) use radio telescopes to listen for alien messages. So far, no one has heard any messages, but the search continues.

Giant radio telescopes like these pick up radio waves from outer space. Perhaps they will pick up messages from aliens!

We aren't just waiting for aliens to call us. We've also sent our own messages into space.

This drawing shows Voyager *1 traveling through space.*

Those messages were sent up in spacecraft. In 1977, the *Voyager 1* and *Voyager 2* were launched. Each carries a recording of sounds and pictures from Earth. If aliens find and play the recordings, it will give them an idea of life on Earth.

Sending a recording into outer space is a little bit like putting a letter in a bottle and throwing it in the ocean. We might never get an answer. Even if we do, it might take a long time to reach us. In fact, *Voyager 1* will take 40,000 years even to get near another star!

What's on the Playlist?

The recordings play sounds from nature, such as the wind, the surf, and bird calls. They include greetings in 55 languages, plus 90 minutes of music. The music ranges from classical to rock 'n' roll, blues, and songs from many cultures.

IMAGINING Aliens

The idea of meeting visitors from other planets is so exciting that many people have made all kinds of shows about aliens.

One of the most famous was a 1938 radio show called "War of the Worlds." It was just a story, but it sounded like a real news report about aliens landing on Earth. Thousands of people believed it and got scared!

Many popular movies have showed scary aliens attacking Earth.

But not all aliens in the movies are terrifying. Some of them are kind of sweet. The 1982 movie *E.T.: The Extraterrestrial* featured a cuddly alien who just wanted to "phone home." In *Close Encounters of the Third Kind*, a man was drawn to a site where aliens were going to land.

Phone home! Big-headed, blue-eyed E.T. made aliens seem cute and cuddly.

On TV, comedian Robin Williams. played a zany alien on *Mork and Mindy*.

Some television shows and movies don't show aliens coming to Earth. Instead, they show people traveling to distant worlds. The crews of the popular *Star Trek* TV series made meeting aliens seem like an exciting adventure. If aliens ever do show up on Earth, they'll sure have fun seeing how we thought they would look and act!

The cast members of the Star Trek *shows and movies became world famous. The series captured popular ideas about the excitement of traveling through outer space.*

GLOSSARY

abductions   kidnappings

aliens   beings from another planet or another part of the universe

astronomers   scientists who study the stars and outer space

bacteria   tiny life forms that are sometimes helpful and sometimes cause disease and are found almost everywhere on Earth

complicated   made up of many different parts, so it is hard to do or understand

encounter   a meeting

extraterrestrial   (E.T.) coming from outside Earth, or outer space

galaxies   large groups of stars and planets

hypnosis   a way of putting people into a sleeplike condition in which they can answer questions, take suggestions, and remember things

metallic   made of metal or similar to metal

telescope   an instrument that makes faraway objects seem closer and brighter

FIND OUT MORE

BOOKS

U.F.O.s and Crop Circles
  by Paul Mason
  (Macmillan, New York) 2005
  This book includes stories about people seeing UFOs, people being "abducted" by aliens, and mysterious crop circles.

U.F.O. Files: Out of This World . . . But True?
  by Sean Plottner
  (Disney Press, New York) 1997
  A longtime kids' writer looks into some of the most famous UFO stories and tries to find the truth.

The U.F.O. Hunter's Handbook
  by Caroline Tiger
  (Price Stern Sloan, New York) 2001.
  Learn tips and techniques for searching out UFOs.

Unidentified Flying Objects and Extra Terrestrial Life
  by Carole Marsh
  (21st Century Books, Fairfield, IA) 1997
  This book includes lists of UFO sightings by state.

WEB SITES

Visit our home page for lots of links about outer space, space travel, aliens, and UFOs: www.childsworld.com/links

Note to Parents, Teachers, and Librarians: We routinely check our Web links to make sure they're safe, active sites—so encourage your readers to check them out!

INDEX

N. B. Grace is a freelance writer, novelist, and playwright. She has written many nonfiction magazine articles for young readers, as well as a book on ghosts. She lives in New York City.